Let's Sled INSTEAD

Anders Hanson

Consulting Editor, Diane Craig, M.A./Reading Specialist

ABDO
Publishing Company

Published by ABDO Publishing Company, 4940 Viking Drive, Edina, Minnesota 55435.

Printed in the United States.

Credits
Edited by: Pam Price
Curriculum Coordinator: Nancy Tuminelly
Cover and Interior Design and Production: Mighty Media
Photo and Illustration Credits: BananaStock Ltd., Corbis Images, Digital Vision, Eyewire Images, Tracy Kompelien, PhotoDisc, Stockbyte

Library of Congress Cataloging-in-Publication Data

Hanson, Anders, 1980-
     Let's sled instead / Anders Hanson.
       p. cm. -- (Rhyme time)
     Includes index.
     ISBN 1-59197-802-5 (hardcover)
     ISBN 1-59197-908-0 (paperback)
     1. English language--Rhyme--Juvenile literature. I. Title. II. Rhyme time (ABDO Publishing Company)

     PE1517.H376 2004
     428.1'3--dc22
                                                                    2004047362

SandCastle™ books are created by a professional team of educators, reading specialists, and content developers around five essential components that include phonemic awareness, phonics, vocabulary, text comprehension, and fluency. All books are written, reviewed, and leveled for guided reading, early intervention reading, and Accelerated Reader® programs and designed for use in shared, guided, and independent reading and writing activities to support a balanced approach to literacy instruction.

Let Us Know

After reading the book, SandCastle would like you to tell us your stories about reading. What is your favorite page? Was there something hard that you needed help with? Share the ups and downs of learning to read. We want to hear from you! To get posted on the ABDO Publishing Company Web site, send us e-mail at:

sandcastle@abdopub.com

SandCastle Level: Transitional

Words that rhyme do not have to be spelled the same. These words rhyme with each other:

red

bed

bread

said

fed

sled

head

spread

led

thread

Louis is sick, so he has to stay in bed.

Abby eats a piece of whole
wheat bread.

Rebecca fed a carrot to
her bunny.

Warren has an apple on
his head.

During practice, Scott led the team across the field.

"Don't tell anyone this secret!"
Neal said.

Mindy, Howard, and Ashley chase the red ball.

Faith spread peanut butter on her toast.

Bonnie and Gaby lie on their **sled**.

Niles strings a red spool on thick, yellow thread.

Let's Sled Instead

14

There is a dog named Ed.
Ed likes to play with
spools of red thread.

"Please don't make
a mess of that thread,"
said Ed's owner, Fred.

"Let's go sled instead!"

Oh, how Ed loves to sled!
Down the hill he sped,
until his hat blew off his head!

Ed has so much fun on the sled
that thoughts of red thread
never enter his head.

After a day on the sled,
Ed wants to be fed.

So Fred gives Ed a big loaf of bread.

Ed is tired and ready for bed.
Ed used to dream of red thread,
but now he dreams of his sled instead.

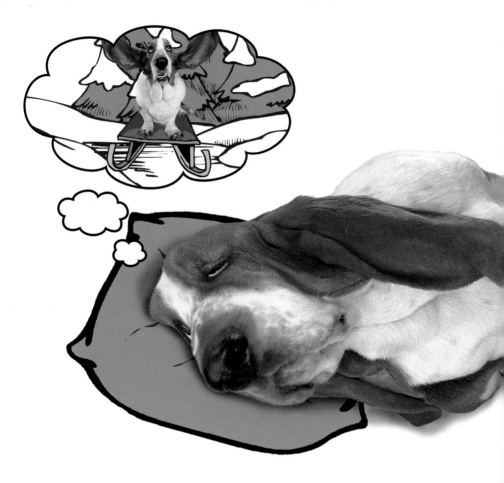

Rhyming Riddle

What do you call
a resting place for loaves?

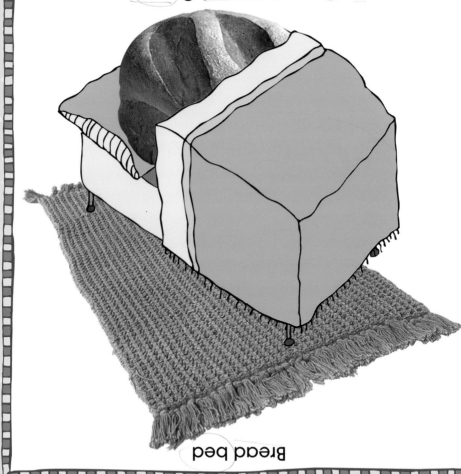

Bread bed

Glossary

led. a small vehicle with runners for travel over ice and snow, especially one used to coast down hills for fun

spool. a cylinder around which a material, such as wire or thread, is wound

spread. to distribute, apply, or cover

hread. a thin strand of material, such as cotton or silk, that is used for sewing

whole wheat. made from entire wheat kernels that are ground up

About SandCastle™

A professional team of educators, reading specialists, and content developers created the SandCastle™ series to support young readers as they develop reading skills and strategies and increase their general knowledge. The SandCastle™ series has four levels that correspond to early literacy development in young children. The levels are provided to help teachers and parents select the appropriate books for young readers.

Emerging Readers
(no flags)

Beginning Readers
(1 flag)

Transitional Readers
(2 flags)

Fluent Readers
(3 flags)

These levels are meant only as a guide. All levels are subject to change.

To see a complete list of SandCastle™ books and other nonfiction titles from ABDO Publishing Company, visit www.abdopub.com or contact us at:
4940 Viking Drive, Edina, Minnesota 55435 • 1-800-800-1312 • fax: 1-952-831-1632